SWINDON

LIVING MEMORIES

BRIAN BRIDGEMAN was born in Swindon in 1936. He was a founder member of The Swindon Society in 1972, and has been the main author of most of the series of 'Swindon in Old Photographs' books published under the Society's name since 1988. Brian is a retired chartered engineer. He has also written several books on the Midland & South Western Junction Railway and on aviation.

FRANCIS FRITH'S
PHOTOGRAPHIC MEMORIES

SWINDON

LIVING MEMORIES

BRIAN BRIDGEMAN

First published in the United Kingdom in 2003 by
Frith Book Company Ltd

Paperback Edition 2003
ISBN 1-85937-656-8

British Library Cataloguing in Publication Data

Francis Frith's Swindon Living Memories
Brian Bridgeman

Frith Book Company Ltd
Frith's Barn, Teffont,
Salisbury, Wiltshire SP3 5QP
Tel: +44 (0) 1722 716 376
Email: info@francisfrith.co.uk
www.francisfrith.co.uk

Printed and bound in Great Britain

Front Cover: Regent Street c1965 S254065

CONTENTS

FRANCIS FRITH
VICTORIAN PIONEER

FRANCIS FRITH, founder of the world-famous photographic archive, was a complex and multi-talented man. A devout Quaker and a highly successful Victorian businessman, he was philosophic by nature and pioneering in outlook.

By 1855 he had already established a wholesale grocery business in Liverpool, and sold it for the astonishing sum of £200,000, which is the equivalent today of over £15,000,000. Now a multi-millionaire, he was able to indulge his passion for travel. As a child he had pored over travel books written by early explorers, and his fancy and imagination had been stirred by family holidays to the sublime mountain regions of Wales and Scotland. 'What a land of spirit-stirring and enriching scenes and places!' he had written. He was to return to these scenes of grandeur in later years to 'recapture the thousands of vivid and tender memories', but with a different purpose. Now in his thirties, and captivated by the new science of photography, Frith set out on a series of pioneering journeys up the Nile and to the Near East that occupied him from 1856 unti 1860.

INTRIGUE AND EXPLORATION

These far-flung journeys were packed with intrigue and adventure. In his life story, written when he was sixty-three, Frith tells of being held captive by bandits, and of fighting 'an awful midnight battle to the very point of surrender with a deadly pack of hungry, wild dogs'. Wearing flowing Arab costume, Frith arrived at Akaba by camel seventy years before Lawrence of Arabia, where he encountered 'desert princes and rival sheikhs, blazing with jewel-hilted swords'.

He was the first photographer to venture beyond the sixth cataract of the Nile. Africa was still the mysterious 'Dark Continent', and Stanley and Livingstone's historic meeting was a decade into the future. The conditions for picture taking confound belief. He laboured for hours in his wicker dark-room in the sweltering heat of the desert, while the volatile chemicals fizzed dangerously in their trays. Back in London he exhibited his photographs and was 'rapturously cheered' by members of the Royal Society. His reputation as a photographer was made overnight.

VENTURE OF A LIFE-TIME

Characteristically, Frith quickly spotted the opportunity to create a new business as a specialist publisher of photographs. He lived in an era of immense and sometimes violent change. For the poor, in the early part of Victoria's reign, work was exhausting and the hours long, and people had precious little free time to enjoy themselves. Most people had no transport other than a cart or gig at their disposal, and rarely

travelled far beyond the boundaries of their own town or village. However, by the 1870s the railways had threaded their way across the country, and Bank Holidays and half-day Saturdays had been made obligatory by Act of Parliament. All of a sudden the working man and his family were able to enjoy days out and see a little more of the world.

With typical business acumen, Francis Frith foresaw that these new tourists would enjoy having souvenirs to commemorate their days out. In 1860 he married Mary Ann Rosling and set out on a new career: his aim was to photograph every city, town and village in Britain. For the next thirty years he travelled the country by train and by pony and trap, producing fine photographs of seaside resorts and beauty spots that were keenly bought by millions of Victorians. These prints were painstakingly pasted into family albums and pored over during the dark nights of winter, rekindling precious memories of summer excursions.

THE RISE OF FRITH & CO

Frith's studio was soon supplying retail shops all over the country. To meet the demand he gathered about him a small team of photographers, and published the work of independent artist-photographers of the calibre of Roger Fenton and Francis Bedford. In order to gain some understanding of the scale of Frith's

business one only has to look at the catalogue issued by Frith & Co in 1886: it runs to some 670 pages, listing not only many thousands of views of the British Isles but also many photographs of most European countries, and China, Japan, the USA and Canada - note the sample page shown here from the hand-written Frith & Co ledgers recording the pictures. By 1890 Frith had created the greatest specialist photographic publishing company in the world, with over 2,000 sales outlets - more than the combined number that Boots and WH Smith have today! The picture on the next page shows the Frith & Co display board at Ingleton in the Yorkshire Dales. Beautifully constructed with mahogany frame and gilt inserts, it could display up to a dozen local scenes.

POSTCARD BONANZA

The ever-popular holiday postcard we know today took many years to develop. In 1870 the Post Office issued the first plain cards, with a pre-printed stamp on one face. In 1894 they allowed other publishers' cards to be sent through the mail with an attached adhesive halfpenny stamp. Demand grew rapidly, and in 1895 a new size of postcard was permitted called the court card, but there was little room for illustration. In 1899, a year after Frith's death, a new card measuring 5.5 x 3.5 inches became the standard format, but it was not until 1902 that the divided back came into being, so that the address and message could be on one face and a full-size illustration on the other. Frith & Co were in the vanguard of postcard development: Frith's sons Eustace and Cyril continued their father's monumental task, expanding the number of views offered to the public and recording more and more places in Britain, as the coasts and countryside were opened up to mass travel.

Francis Frith had died in 1898 at his villa in Cannes, his great project still growing. The archive he created continued in business for another seventy years. By 1970 it contained over a third of a million pictures showing 7,000 British towns and villages.

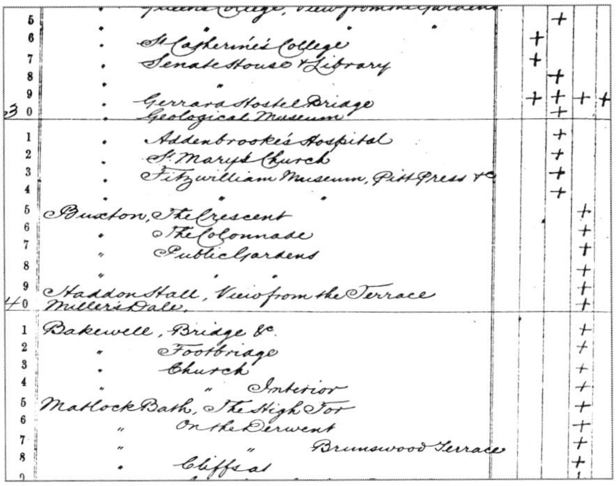

A handwritten ledger list appears at the top left, with entries such as:

- St Catherine's College
- Senate House & Library
- Gerrard Hostel Bridge
- Geological Museum
- Addenbrooke's Hospital
- St Mary's Church
- Fitzwilliam Museum, Pitt Press &c
- Buxton, The Crescent
- The Colonnade
- Public Gardens
- Haddon Hall, View from the Terrace
- Miller's Dale
- Bakewell, Bridge &c.
- Footbridge
- Church
- Interior
- Matlock Bath, The High Tor
- On the Derwent
- Brunswood Terrace
- Cliffe &c

FRANCIS FRITH'S LEGACY

Frith's legacy to us today is of immense significance and value, for the magnificent archive of evocative photographs he created provides a unique record of change in the cities, towns and villages throughout Britain over a century and more. Frith and his fellow studio photographers revisited locations many times down the years to update their views, compiling for us an enthralling and colourful pageant of British life and character.

We are fortunate that Frith was dedicated to recording the minutiae of everyday life. For it is this sheer wealth of visual data, the painstaking chronicle of changes in dress, transport, street layouts, buildings, housing, engineering and landscape that captivates us so much today. His remarkable images offer us a powerful link with the past and with the lives of our ancestors.

THE VALUE OF THE ARCHIVE TODAY

Computers have now made it possible for Frith's many thousands of images to be accessed almost instantly. Frith's images are increasingly used as visual resources, by social historians, by researchers into genealogy and ancestry, by architects and town planners, and by teachers involved in local history projects.

In addition, the archive offers every one of us an opportunity to examine the places where we and our families have lived and worked down the years. Highly successful in Frith's own era, the archive is now, a century and more on, entering a new phase of popularity. Historians consider the Francis Frith Collection to be of prime national importance. It is the only archive of its kind remaining in private ownership. Francis Frith's archive is now housed in an historic timber barn in the beautiful village of Teffont in Wiltshire. Its founder would not recognize the archive office as it is today. In place of the many thousands of dusty boxes containing glass plate negatives and an all-pervading odour of photographic chemicals, there are now ranks of computer screens. He would be amazed to watch his images travelling round the world at unimaginable speeds through internet lines.

The archive's future is both bright and exciting. Francis Frith, with his unshakeable belief in making photographs available to the greatest number of people, would undoubtedly approve of what is being done today with his lifetime's work. His photographs depicting our shared past are now bringing pleasure and enlightenment to millions around the world a century and more after his death.

SWINDON
AN INTRODUCTION

TWO HUNDRED years ago, Swindon was a quiet and almost unknown market town on a hill in rural north Wiltshire. Although mentioned in the Domesday Book, the small settlement only had a population of 1,198 in 1801, at the time of the first official census, slightly less than the neighbouring towns of Wootton Bassett (1,244), Cricklade (1,333) and considerably smaller than Highworth, which then boasted a population of 2,328.

In the 1830s the Great Western Railway laid its tracks through the green fields about one and a half miles to the north of the old town close to the route of the Wilts & Berks Canal. Here, the brilliant engineer Isambard Kingdom Brunel established his workshops along with housing for the workers. A church (St Mark's) and a school were also built with funds subscribed by shareholders of the railway company. In addition, some enlightened welfare projects were set up by the GWR, including a Medical Fund Society to provide medical

and other care for the railwaymen and their families, which in many ways anticipated the Welfare State of today. To encourage adult education, the company also built the Mechanics Institute in the heart of the community. This provided evening classes for railwaymen and women, a reading room, a lending library and a programme of lectures, debates, drama and other entertainment.

By the 1850s the New Town was larger than its old neighbour on the hill. The two towns gradually grew together over the next fifty years, and finally, in January 1900, they joined together as one municipal borough. In due course, Mr G J Churchward, Manager of the Works and later Chief Mechanical Engineer of the GWR, became the first mayor. The population of the town was then around 45,000. Eventually some 14,000 were employed at the giant complex of the GWR works, and Swindon became known throughout the world as a railway town. The works not only provided the majority of the employment for Swindon itself for many years, but also for much of the working population of the surrounding area, which was connected to the town by railway and road transport links. The remainder of the inhabitants of the area also depended on the railway to a large extent, providing the essential services and products required by those who worked 'inside' (a local term for those who spent their working lives confined within the walls of the railway works) and their families. For the then limited leisure time of Swindonians, the council developed the site of former quarries in the Old Town into the Town Gardens; and Coate Water, originally created as a reservoir for the Wilts & Berks canal, became one of the town's most attractive and well used open spaces.

Until 1919, Swindon did not have its own Member of Parliament, being in the parliamentary division of Cricklade. The town continued to expand. In October 1928 the borough boundaries were extended by annexation of the whole of the rural parish of Rodbourne Cheney and parts of Stratton St Margaret, so that the whole of the first council housing estate in the area, Pinehurst, came within the borough. Districts that formed parts of several other adjoining parishes – Wroughton, Chiseldon, Lydiard Millicent and Lydiard Tregoze - were also included within the new borough boundaries. At that time the total population of Swindon was some 65,000.

The 1930s brought much unemployment and hardship to the area. In 1937, however, a new Deputy Town Clerk was appointed for Swindon. His name was David Murray John, at that time only 29 years of age. From 1938, until a few weeks before his death in 1974, he was Town Clerk. Educated at Huddersfield College and Oxford, where he read history, Murray John soon realised the dangers for a town then virtually dependent for its economic livelihood upon the single industry of the railway. The Second World War and the 1950s brought several large engineering companies to Swindon or the immediate neighbourhood, including Vickers-Armstrong, the Plessey Company and Pressed Steel Fisher Limited. All these companies required many workers. The 1952 Town Development Act gave Swindon the opportunity to bid for further expansion. Murray John and his council colleagues set out to 'sell' Swindon with unflagging energy in boardrooms and offices throughout the land. They won the faith of London councillors charged with re-settling large number of families. Soon 20,000 people and some industries were received; 9,000 houses were built within the borough boundary, including the estates of Penhill and Walcot. In 1961 permission was given to build outside the boundary. In 1974, an extensive reorganisation was carried out throughout England and Wales, and the whole of the Highworth Rural District area was united with the old Borough of Swindon. The new authority became the Borough of Thamesdown, although some of the responsibilities, including education and library services, were transferred to Wiltshire County Council. Subsequently, further expansion to the west and recently to the north has resulted in the incorporation of parts of parishes formerly administered by the Cricklade and Wootton Bassett Rural District Council and then, from 1974, the North Wiltshire Council.

To cater for the cultural needs of the townsfolk, the Corporation of Swindon bought the house and estate of Lydiard Park from Lord Bolingbroke in 1943. This has been developed over the years as a conference centre, a recreation area and a site for large outdoor concerts and Shakespearean productions. The mansion itself, a splendid classical building, was extensively restored and refurbished and opened to the public in 1955. Since then there has been an ongoing programme to find and restore the original St John furnishings, silver, china, glassware and other artefacts. The picture collection of the 6th Viscount Bolingbroke was also purchased by Swindon Corporation for permanent display in the house. After the Second

COMMERCIAL ROAD *c1965* S254067

World War the former grounds of the Lawn manor house in the Old Town were purchased, and have been kept as a natural and delightful park; also, the ruins of Swindon's medieval parish church, Holy Rood, were restored in a simple but dignified manner. Using funds donated for the Coronation celebrations in 1953, Queen's Park was laid out in the centre of Swindon close by to Regent Circus and the Town Hall.

The opening of the M4 motorway to the south of Swindon in the early 1970s, with its links to other motorways and arterial routes, led to a further expansion in employment opportunities within the area. Although the railway works closed finally in 1986, and other engineering companies have now left the town, the establishment of the Honda UK car assembly and of an engine manufacturing plant at South Marston, on the old Vickers airfield site, has enabled Swindon to maintain a high level of employment in the area. Over the years many major national companies have also established their headquarters within the town, including W H Smith, Castrol UK and the Nationwide Building Society. Its attractive environment has also resulted in English Heritage, the National Monuments Record Centre and, in the near future, the National Trust establishing their main offices in Swindon.

Attempts to gain city status for Swindon began in the 1990s, but by 2002 its bid had twice been rejected. Unfortunately, despite the commercial success engendered in recent years, the town's cultural life and infrastructure have not developed to the same level. Action is now under way, however, to address many of the faults. A new railway museum, Steam, to celebrate the GWR works and the men who worked there, opened in 2000. A new hospital, the Great Western, opened in December 2002 close to Junction 15 of the M4 to replace the aging Princess Margaret Hospital; the University of Bath in Swindon has been established at Oakfield Campus; and a start has been made towards the possible restoration of the derelict former GWR Mechanics' Institute. The regeneration of the Old Town is also under way after many years of neglect, and ambitious proposals have been presented for the restoration of the historic Lydiard Park over the next few years. A draft local plan is also being drawn up as a basis for town centre regeneration whilst protecting the best of the Borough's natural environment.

In April 1997, the former Thamesdown Borough Council became a new unitary authority known as the Borough of Swindon; its population in 2002 was 181,000. Some of the surrounding small towns and villages, where life has, in many ways, continued unchanged, often feel threatened by the continual expansion of Swindon. The northern residential development towards Blunsdon has added to their concerns: this began in the late 1990s, with its aim to provide eventually an additional 10,000 homes. Another concern is the existing proposals for building to the southwest of the borough in the so-called 'front garden'. Existing Government policy requires Swindon to find room for nearly 7,500 more houses by 2011. Some inhabitants of the largely rural county of Wiltshire look on Swindon with its tower blocks and industrial and housing estates with disfavour. However, the town is still a magnet which draws many people from all over north Wiltshire to earn their living there and to use its many leisure and recreational facilities.

SWINDON
THE OLD TOWN

VICTORIA ROAD AND CHRIST CHURCH
c1950 S254025

Victoria Street is first mentioned in the 1848 Kelly's Directory; it extended only from Bath Road to the junction with Prospect Place we see here in the foreground. A new section to connect this junction with the New Town centre was constructed by 1875, and later, in 1903, the combined route was renamed Victoria Road. Immediately to the left today, in Prospect Place, stands the studios of BBC Radio Swindon.

CHRIST CHURCH
1948 S254018

'The Old Lady on the Hill', the parish church of the Old Town, was designed by Sir George Gilbert Scott, the eminent Victorian architect, who had previously provided the design for the railway church of St Mark's in the GWR Railway Village; he also designed the Albert Memorial and the St Pancras Hotel in London. Christ Church was built and opened in 1851 to replace the medieval church of Holy Rood, which was by then too small for the growing population of Old Town. Its tower and broached spire (approximately 150ft in height) are based on the 13th-century church of Buckworth, near Huntingdon, according to John Betjeman, who wrote a poem celebrating the famous peal of bells from this well-loved building on Swindon's skyline.

WOOD STREET *c1950*
S254022
Looking East

Wood Street dates back many centuries – the lease of a tenement dated 1599 is the earliest reference. It was also known in the past as Windmill Street (according to the writer Richard Jefferies), after a corn-mill which had once stood here, and as Blacksmith's Street. The shop fronts to the left today are hardly changed. The tobacconist, George E Morris, is now the Victoria Bookshop. Edward Bay's (note the sign beyond on the left) were heating engineers and general ironmongers. Their large premises later became the Co-op Discount store. It is now divided into several shops and stores. On the right stands the Cross Keys public house, which has recently been completely modernized and renamed Picklejohn's.

▼ **THE GODDARD ARMS, HIGH STREET** *c1950* S254014
Looking East from Wood Street

An inn has stood on this site for 400 years. It was known as the Crown until about 1810, when it was renamed in honour of the Goddard family, the lords of the manor of High Swindon. The Magistrates' Court for Swindon was held here until the Old Town Hall was built in the Market Square in 1852. In April 1914, Francis Priscilla Hunter, aged 23, a between-maid here, was shot dead by her jealous lover, Walter James White. He was executed for the murder at Winchester in June 1914.

▼ **HIGH STREET AND THE GODDARD ARMS** *c1950* S254023

This view, looking north, shows the Goddard Arms to the right. The old Automobile Association cast-iron signpost standing at this former major road junction has long since gone. On the left we can see Barclay's Bank, on the corner of Cricklade Street. This building opened as the Wiltshire & Dorset Bank in 1885 and is now used as offices and as a hairdresser's salon.

▲**HIGH STREET, LOOKING NORTH** *c1950* S254024
Looking North

The main street of Old Swindon was first recorded in 1581. On the left stands the Bell Hotel, established, according to the wording over the door, in 1515; it was the departure point for the tri-weekly London coach from Swindon, and the post office in the 1830s. The Victorian shop-front of the chemist next to the hotel has now gone - the premises have been taken into an extension and courtyard for the hotel, which has been changed almost beyond recognition in recent years. It is now known as Fusion, with extra residential bedrooms and a Thai restaurant. The depot of H & G Symonds Ltd (further down the road) was the former North Wilts Brewery. Later used as an area office by Courage until 1978, the whole site has now been redeveloped as the main local branch of Barclay's Bank, although the original façade has been retained.

HIGH STREET *1948* S254012
Looking South to Marlborough Road

The buildings to the left stood next to the Old Town Hall on the Market Square. In the 19th century the shop on the corner was a grocer's and baker's owned by the family of the writer Richard Jefferies. The Masons Arms (beyond), with its own stables, which stood opposite the junction with Newport Street, had parts of the building dating back to the late 17th century. Immediately adjacent to this inn in Marlborough Road was another old public house, the Bell & Shoulder of Mutton. This section of the High Street has changed beyond recognition today. Road widening in 1969-70 swept away all the buildings to the left; the HSBC Bank complex, and its adjacent car park, now cover the area.

QUARRY ROAD TENNIS COURTS
c1955 S254037

These municipal tennis courts stand close by the Town
Gardens and were constructed off the old access road
between the two main stone quarries after the development
of the Gardens. They are still much used today –especially
during and immediately after the Wimbledon fortnight!

SWINDON TOWN STATION *1961* S254535

This photograph was taken on 10 September 1961, the last day of passenger services on the former Midland & South Western Junction Railway line that connected Andoversford (near Cheltenham) to Andover and the south. The station, opened in 1881, was situated off Newport Street near the junction with Devizes Road. The M & SWJR was taken over by the Great Western Railway under the Railways Act of 1923. During both World Wars this vitally important strategic route carried an immense amount of military traffic north and south. After World War II, however, traffic reduced, and the line was closed along with many other country routes. The photograph shows the Railway Correspondence & Travel Society Tour train in the station – one of two special trains that ran that day over the line for the benefit of railway enthusiasts. Today the site of the station is the Central Trading Estate, with light industrial units, and the route of the line between the station and west Swindon is a pleasant cycle and pedestrian path.

TOWN GARDENS AND COATE WATER

TOWN GARDENS *c1955* S254042
The Park Keeper's Lodge and the Aviary

The gardens were laid out in the late 19th century on the site of old Purbeck stone quarries formerly owned by the Goddard family. These quarries had given Swindon an important industry long before the arrival of the GWR, for the stone was considered of excellent quality. In 1893 the Old Swindon Local Board purchased the quarries, and the gardens were opened in May 1894 by Mr W Reynolds, Chairman of the Board. The park keeper's lodge in the centre of the photograph is adjacent to the main entrance to the gardens from Westlecot Road. The aviary to the left was built in 1928; it remained here until it was replaced by a new decorative black iron construction to the east of the pond in 1994 as part of the Town Gardens centenary celebrations. The birds have always been a very popular attraction for local children.

TOWN GARDENS *c1955* S254043
The Pathway to the Bandstand

This cherry tree-lined main central path runs north from the southern entrance in Westlecot Road. In spring the blossom on the trees is a beautiful sight, and the flower beds are alive with tulips and other spring flowers. The flowers are changed twice each year, so that through the summer and autumn families can take their ease on the lawns and enjoy the pleasures of this lovely spot. In the background, the pathway leads uphill via steps in a planted rockery. Today the gardens still retain their feeling of their original Victorian splendour.

TOWN GARDENS *1948* S254020
The Goldfish Pond from the South

This portion of the gardens is situated near the south-eastern arm of the perimeter path. It was in what was called the 'children's corner' when the gardens opened in 1894. The goldfish pond was originally oval in shape, and formerly contained a single-spray bronze fountain known as the Water Carrier on a small island. It was reworked in the late 1920s to the shape we now see today. The pond was renovated for the centenary celebrations in the 1990s, and recently a new fountain has been installed.

▼ **TOWN GARDENS** *c1955* S254041
The Goldfish Pond from the North

Another view of the goldfish pond. Again, mothers with their young children are enjoying their afternoon in this peaceful spot. Today the modern aviary stands in the area to the left of this photograph.

► **TOWN GARDENS**
The Bandstand c1955
S254040

We are looking towards the bandstand across the lawn and rockery from the south. In the early days there were six full-time gardeners employed in the Town Gardens; today there are only two full-time skilled workers, with three others on call, together with three volunteers.

◄TOWN GARDENS
The Bandstand
c1955 S254044

The decorative cast iron octagonal bandstand was an original feature. It stands amidst semicircular flower beds, and forms the focal point of the gardens. Originally it only had a simple cast iron weather vane on the top; the clock, provided by Messrs Allan of Glasgow, and the turret were added in 1927. When this photograph was taken, seating was installed; but since then the bandstand has resumed its original purpose, and is used as the venue for weekly Sunday band concerts in the summer months.

► TOWN GARDENS *c1955*
S254039
The Bandstand and the Refreshment Kiosk

The bandstand is situated close to the refreshment kiosk (right). This small octagonal building itself has an interesting history. It was built in the GWR Works in 1914 as an advertising trade stand, and appeared in many large agricultural and other exhibitions all over the country – it was easy to erect and could be carried in a normal railway wagon. In 1942, after lying unused for years in the GWR stores, it was purchased by the Borough Council and erected in the Town Gardens as a café.

▶ **TOWN GARDENS**
The Entrance to the
Concert Bowl c1955
S254038

This rectangular
garden at the heart
of the gardens, with
its formally planted
flower beds, leads to
the entrance porch
of the Concert Bowl
with its iron
turnstiles. Both the
Concert Bowl and
entrance were
designed by J B L
Thompson (the
Borough Surveyor at
the time) in 1934-36
and opened in May
1936.

◀ **TOWN GARDENS**
1948 S254017
The Concert Bowl
Open-Air Theatre

The Art Deco Concert
Bowl is situated in a
valley that was the
former main quarry
area. It is one of only a
handful built in this
country in this style. In
the 1990s the Concert
Bowl was restored with
the support of Burmah
Castrol plc, and is now
the venue for regular
summer concerts and
drama productions.

▲ **TOWN GARDENS** *The Rose Gardens 1948* S254011

Situated west of the Concert Bowl, the rose gardens were laid out in the late 1920s-early 1930s on the site of a former maze. The many roses in the garden provide a varied mixture of scent and colour throughout the summer. The small sculpture of Pan was later moved to a new position on the lawn south of the rose gardens. The octagonal seat shown in the background was removed in later years.

◄ **COATE WATER** *c1955*
S254036
Looking West to the Diving Board

Coate Water was originally constructed in 1821-22 as a reservoir, and was designed to overcome water shortages on the canal system around the town when the North Wilts Canal had opened in 1819. In 1914 Swindon Borough Council purchased both Coate Water and sections of disused canal within the town. Since this time, it has been built up to be a major attraction for local people.

COATE WATER *The Diving Board c1950* S254013

The concrete diving stage was designed by J B L Thompson, and was officially opened at a gala in June 1935. One of the celebrities giving a demonstration on this occasion was Miss Cicely Cousins, who had won the ASA High Diving Championship in 1934. Sad to say, since swimming was stopped owing to pollution of the lake, the structure has not been used.

AROUND SWINDON TOWN CENTRE

VICTORIA ROAD *c1955* S254056
Looking North

The Swindon and North Wilts Technical Institute building (now known as the College) is on the left. This was built in 1896 at a cost of £10,000 on land presented by W V Rolleston. At the bottom of the hill is the domed building of the Central Hall (originally built as the Wesleyan Central Mission Hall in 1907); how sad that it was demolished in 1985 to make way for an office block, Kingsbridge Point.

VICTORIA ROAD TO REGENT CIRCUS
c1955 S254035

This section of Victoria Road was the scene of the famous tram crash in June 1906, which resulted in five deaths and a large number injured. Owing to the lack of insurance cover, the local rates were raised to cover the compensation awarded. The small local shops of this period have been mostly replaced by restaurants and fast-food outlets.

VICTORIA ROAD *c1965* S254096
We are looking towards the imposing building of the Presbyterian church in the distance and Groundwell Road. The small, busy, individually owned shops of this period have now disappeared; they have become mostly restaurants with an Indian theme and fast food outlets - and one is a topless dancing bar.

THE PRESBYTERIAN CHURCH, VICTORIA ROAD
c1965 extract from S254096

The church was built in 1899 to a design by William Wallace of London. The Trinity Presbyterian Church (as it was known at this time) had seating for 400. By 1990 the upkeep of the building and the falling numbers in the congregation resulted in them moving to the Pilgrim Centre in Regent Circus. The building is now used by the Toad Hall children's day nursery.

GROUNDWELL ROAD *c1955* S254052

This fine view looks from the junction with Victoria Road, with Holy Rood Roman Catholic church on the right. The second shop (with the awning in position) near the junction with Wells Street is now one of the most picturesque shops in the town, with its large display of fruit and vegetables along the pavement, as well as its fish display in the window.

HOLY ROOD ROMAN CATHOLIC CHURCH, GROUNDWELL ROAD c1955 extract from
S254052

The church, designed by the architect E Doran Webb, was officially opened in May 1905. The new building enabled the congregation to move from premises they used at Regent Circus, which had previously been used as a nonconformist chapel. The Roman Catholic school next to the church had been in use since 1899. The church was greatly extended in 1969-70 by building a new nave on the site of, but at right angles to, the old one.

THE GARDEN OF REMEMBRANCE, GROUNDWELL ROAD c1955 S254049

These gardens in Groundwell Road were officially opened on 15 November 1950 by HRH Princess Elizabeth on her visit to the town. The creator of the Queens Park concept was Maurice Williams, in his role as General Superintendent of Parks in Swindon. During 1997 a rededication service took place, when new granite plaques were put alongside those of the official opening ceremony on the entrance gateway.

QUEENS PARK *c1955* S254048

Since its official opening in Coronation year (1953) by Sir Noel Arkell, this area in the centre of the town has been known as Queens Park. It was developed from clay pits left over from old brickworks; it had formerly been the site of earthworks for an ill-founded attempt to excavate a tunnel through Swindon hill for the Swindon, Marlborough & Andover Railway in 1875-76.

▶ QUEENS PARK
c1960 S254057

A crazy paving pathway meanders its way amongst a rockery within the park. We can see the roofs of houses lining Hunt Street at the rear.

▼ QUEENS PARK
c1965 S254069

Here we see the corner section of the lake, with the path leading up to the entrance gateway at Durham Street. Over the years this section (at the position of the couple in the centre admiring the flower display) has seen many changes. This includes a seated shelter, which today is covered in modern-day graffiti.

▶ QUEENS PARK
c1965 S254068
Looking North

This is our initial view of the park as we enter from the Durham Street gateway. In the summer many lunchtime office workers seeking solace and tranquillity use this entrance to leave the hustle and noise of the centre of town for a short period.

◄ QUEENS PARK
c1955 S254046
Looking West

We are looking across the lake to the houses in Durham Street, with the Presbyterian church roof in the centre of the picture, and the Holy Rood Roman Catholic church on the right. The vegetation on the far bank has now grown to fill the open spaces shown here, giving the whole site an impression of being far removed from the centre of a busy and thriving town.

EUCLID STREET

c1955 S254053

This view looks down towards the Civic Offices (behind the trees on the left) and the junction with Lincoln Street on the right. The terraced housing in this street originates from the late 1890s, when both houses and a school were built. It seems appropriate that the name Euclid (a Greek mathematician) was used, for there are two schools within a short distance of each other (the other is Clarence Street School).

THE CIVIC OFFICES *1948* S254015

By the middle 1930s the Borough Council had outgrown the offices at the Town Hall, and departments were housed in various buildings around the town. It was decided to use a small recreation ground in Euclid Street, and building took place to a design by Messrs Bertram, Bertram & Rice of Oxford. The offices were officially opened in July 1938 by HRH the Duke of Gloucester.

THE CIVIC OFFICES, EUCLID STREET *1948* S254019

Here we have a picturesque view through the trees towards the Civic Offices in Euclid Street. The offices have suffered the same fate as the Town Hall - they have become too small for the intended council work with the massive expansion of Swindon. The building is still used for council meetings and select committees, and is also now licensed for marriages to take place in the council chamber.

THE TOWN HALL
AND
REGENT CIRCUS

THE TOWN HALL AND THE CENTRAL LIBRARY
c1955 S254034

Swindon adopted the Public Libraries Act in 1942, and its first public library opened in McIlroy's departmental store in Regent Street the following year. The library was later transferred to the former electricity showrooms in Regent Circus in 1946 (see photograph S254062, opposite). A new 'temporary' main lending library was built at the rear of the Town Hall and opened by the author Compton Mackenzie in March 1949. These buildings were given a face lift in the late 1960s, but Swindon is still waiting for a new permanent library.

REGENT CIRCUS
1961 S254063

Through the trees to the left stand the buildings of the Central Library. In the middle distance is the head post office of Swindon at this time, standing on the corner of Princes Street. This was built in 1900 and demolished c1970 to make way for modern offices and shops. The building with the windows in the roof was the Constitutional Conservative Club.

THE COLLEGE, REGENT CIRCUS *1961* S254062

At the centre of the photograph stands the then new College building. At centre right a Bristol bus (Service No 65 to Chippenham) is leaving Rolleston Street with the Bristol Omnibus Company offices on the corner. To the left stands the Art Deco building of the Islington Furnishing Co. This had previously been the Electricity Authority showrooms and public library. It is now Rudi's Bar.

▼ REGENT CIRCUS AND THE COLLEGE *c1965* S254088

Here we have another view of this busy area. Swindonians are taking in the summer sunshine in the seating around the Central Library. The furniture showrooms to the left are empty. As happens today on empty buildings, the windows are already covered in fly-posters for pop group concerts.

▼ THE COLLEGE *c1965* S254087

Connected to the old Technical College in Victoria Road (see page 31), this building was designed by Charles Pike & Partners and officially opened by HRH Prince Philip, Duke of Edinburgh, in April 1961. To the right is Rolleston Street, itself soon to be built over with an extension to the building and a car park in 1966-69. Plans are in hand at present for the complete redevelopment of this area with a new site for the College elsewhere in the town.

▲ **REGENT CIRCUS AND COMMERCIAL ROAD** *1961* S254061
Looking West towards Commercial Road

To the right is the Central Library. The old terrace of shops to the left include
J N Read & Son, butchers. Next to these premises, by the bus stop, stands the sports
shop of Harold Fleming, the famous footballer who played for Swindon Town from
1907-24; he was capped for England eleven times. Fleming Way is named after him.
This whole terrace of shops was later demolished for new buildings.

COMMERCIAL ROAD
c1965 S254067
Looking West

This view looks down Commercial Road towards the old market site. The street at this time was largely occupied by small businesses such as (on the right) Harold the jeweller's, with next door Hiscock's the builder and decorator's. On the opposite corner of the Morley Street junction was Taymac the builders' merchants (now the site of the West Bromwich Building Society).

▶ THE TOWN HALL
c1965 S254092

This was designed by Brightwen Binyon of Ipswich, and opened in October 1891 by the Marquis of Bath as the new public offices building for Swindon. By the 1930s it had become too small and was replaced by the Civic Offices in Euclid Street (see photograph S254015, page38). Swindon Reference Library is still sited here, as it has been since 1949. The main hall of the building is now used as dance studios.

◀ REGENT CIRCUS AND REGENT STREET *c1965*
S254089

By this time this photograph was taken, new offices and shops had replaced the majority of the small shops. A zebra crossing now helps pedestrians to cross the road close by the Cenotaph. A kind policeman is helping a young girl to step safely off the kerb to the left. As in many of the views included in this book, note the bicycle propped on the kerb to the right – probably not needing a lock at this time!

▲ REGENT CIRCUS AND REGENT STREET *c1950*
S254021

At the centre of this photograph stands the Cenotaph. This replaced a temporary wooden structure and was unveiled in October 1920 to commemorate the fallen of World War I. In the background the view is dominated by the giant classical portico of the Baptist Tabernacle. On the corner of Temple Street, next to the Tabernacle, are the Gas Board showrooms, now Circle 7 general store. Note the lack of traffic in this view.

◄ THE BAPTIST TABERNACLE
c1965 extract from S254089

The Baptist Tabernacle was designed by W H Read and opened in 1886. This impressive structure cost £6,000 and had seating for 1,000. Constructed of Bath stone, the colonnade of six Tuscan columns supported a large pediment. It is most regrettable that the building was demolished in 1978; the site was bare until the new Pilgrim Centre was constructed and opened in 1990. The stones of the columns and pediments of the Tabernacle, however, exist to this day in a nursery garden near Tetbury.

THE TOWN HALL *c1965* S254086
Looking South

This view of the Town Hall shows the main entrance at the
centre. In recent years gardens in front of the building, and
front steps leading to the entrance, have been replaced by
steps to the side and an access ramp. Unfortunately, in
building these, the commemorative plaque of the opening in
1891 was covered over! Many election results were
announced to the citizens of Swindon from the balcony over
the doorway. On the wide pavement, centre right, we can see
the small office which was used by the bus inspectors.

REGENT STREET TO FARINGDON ROAD

REGENT STREET *c1965* S254065
Looking towards the Town Hall

It is a busy summer's day in the 1960s. At this time traffic was still allowed in one direction up Regent Street, with parking varying from one side to the other depending on the day of the week. The Baptist Tabernacle and the Gas Board showrooms are to the right, whilst on the left stands the red brick Riflemans Hotel, which dates from 1888. Today the Victorian brick building has been painted an overall cream colour, but unusually in these days, it retains its original name.

▶ **REGENT CIRCUS**
c1955 S254054
*The View North
from the Town Hall*

This view, taken from the Town Hall, shows the layout of Regent Circus leading to Regent Street in the 1950s. The classical portico of the Baptist Tabernacle on the left was enhanced by the flight of stone steps which ran the entire width of the frontage. To the right, small shops including Avonweir, a greengrocer, and Bell Bros, footwear, are to be seen lining the street.

◀ **REGENT STREET** *1948* S254009
The View North-West

This thoroughfare was originally lined with workers' cottages, but from about 1865 many of these dwellings were converted into shops. The small shop fronts to the left were built out from the original terraced houses. On the far left is the Regent Street Primitive Methodist church; it had been built here in 1876 to replace two former chapels on the same site of 1849 and 1863. In 1895 a large Sunday school was built behind the chapel. This remained for many years, even after the chapel itself was demolished in 1957. It served for some years as Swindon's first arts centre and as the children's library.

▲ **REGENT STREET** *1961* S254066
The View North from the ABC Cinema

By this time the view had much changed from that of 1948. To the left, Pearl Assurance House had been built on the site of the Primitive Methodist Church with the Co-operative furniture store underneath the offices. The Royal Wiltshire Bacon Co still stood on the corner to the alley to Regent Place at the centre of the photograph. On the right is the Art Deco ABC Cinema, designed by W R Glen, which opened in February 1937. It changed its name to the Cannon in 1986, but closed in 1991. Today the building is J D Wetherspoon's Savoy bar.

◄ **McILROY'S DEPARTMENTAL STORE, REGENT STREET**
1948 extract from S254009

William McIlroy's store, with its ornate clock tower (built in 1904 by John Norman), was a landmark in this area of Swindon for many years. It was the complete shopping experience for generations of Swindonians. The store had a elegant stairway between the ground and first floors, which was said to have come from an ocean liner. The clock tower and the Edwardian frontage were demolished during refurbishment of the store in c1960, but later some attempt was made to reintroduce the period look to the store windows. However, the store closed in the 1990s, and the whole area was redeveloped as separate units. A new clock tower was built in 1999.

▼ **REGENT STREET** *1967* s254101
The View North-West

Little has changed in this view from that of s254066 (previous page), apart from the frontage of the ABC Cinema. The brick and stone Royal Wilts Bacon Co's shop is today the Borough of Swindon Information Centre. All Regent Street into Bridge Street is now paved over for pedestrian access only.

▼ **REGENT STREET,** *The View North-West 1961* s254363

To the left we can see some of the frontages of the small shops built out from the original cottages. Charles Cycle Co, The Spot, 60 Regent Street, is where many generations of Swindon's youth purchased their models, cycles and sports equipment until its closure in 1979. The Spot is now the premises of Swiss Chalet, a baker and café. In the foreground a friendly member of the constabulary helps a visitor to find his way around Swindon's shopping area.

▲ **REGENT STREET** *c1965* S254064
The View North-West

This view appears to postdate S254363 on page 52 (the 'No Waiting' road markings
have been removed). To the left is The Spot, with Macfisheries, the fishmongers, to its
right. Just beyond stands the slab-sided block of the redeveloped McIlroy's
department store. On the right, next to the Woolworth's store, is James Walker,
jewellers. A jeweller has stood on this site for many years, and still does today.

REGENT STREET *c1955*
S254029
The View South-East

F W Woolworth & Co Ltd
stands on the left next to
James Walker, jeweller. The
first Woolworth's store was
built on the site of
Swindon's first permanent
cinema, the County
Electric Pavilion, in the
1920s. The store was
greatly extended from its
original size in the mid
1930s by taking over the
site of the adjacent
Artillery Arms public
house. To the right we can
see the elegant Edwardian
frontage of William
McIlroy's store.

REGENT STREET *c1950* S254008
The View to Bridge Street

This section of Regent Street is immediately to the north of the McIlroy's store. On the corner of Havelock Street and to the left stood Anstiss & Co Ltd, drapers, which stood here until the 1960s when it suffered two major fires, the second of which destroyed the premises completely. On the right is the Arcadia Cinema, which later became the Classic cartoon cinema. The HMV store now stands on this site. At centre-right is Morse's department store, 10/12 Regent Street. This was the second of Swindon's major stores for many years (with McIlroy's) and was owned by the Morse family of Old Town. W H Smith has occupied this site from 1973.

BRIDGE STREET *c1950* S254006
The View South-East from the Junction with Fleet Street

On this quiet day around 1950 there was practically no traffic.
On the left is Montague Burton, the men's tailors. It had been
built here in the early 1930s on the site of an old public
house, the Oxford Hotel. On the right is Stead & Simpson,
shoe retailers, with Foster Brothers, menswear, next door.
Further up Bridge Street we can see the signs for Timothy
Whites, chemists, and Olivers shoes, with Lipton, the grocers,
on the left. In the distance is the clock tower of McIlroy's
store. Many of the premises in the area are now bars or fast-
food establishments.

▶ **BRIDGE STREET** *c1955* S254030
The View South-East

This view is little changed from
S254006 (previous page). A group of
young men of fashion are keen to
show off their new suits to the
photographer outside Burton's
store. In later years the premises
became Beatties toyshop, and it is
now a bar/restaurant, the
Bedroom. This junction was the
tram centre, with branches leading
off to Old Town, left to Gorse Hill
and right to Rodbourne. The clock
above Stead & Simpson's shop was
used by the tram drivers to check
their timing. Wilkinson's hardware
store now stands where Stead &
Simpson then stood. The old
phoenix plaque above the clock
was saved, and replaced in the new
development in a similar position.

◀ FLEET STREET *c1955*
S254026

We are looking north-east from Fleet Street towards Milford Street, with the junction of Bridge Street to the right. Next to Burton's store stands the original bookshop of W H Smith, 53 Fleet Street, which opened here in 1925. On the extreme left is Peacocks, the drapers. The building had been the Central Cinema from 1912 for about thirty years. Peacocks remained trading from here until recent years. On the corner of the northern section of Bridge Street stands Lennard's shoe shop.

FARINGDON ROAD *c1955* S254032
Looking North-East to Fleet Street

The junction to East Street is on the left, with Catherine Street on the right. The stone building seen partway down Fleet Street on the left is the Sir Daniel Arms, named in honour of Sir Daniel Gooch. In later years it was renamed the Sportsman. Adjacent to the public house was the range of New Swindon Co-operative Society shops, comprising menswear, footwear, shoe repairs, drapery, confectionery and grocery stores. The majority of these premises were completely demolished in later years, and an open-air market was held here. In recent times, however, the whole area to the left has been completely redeveloped for two large bar/restaurants, and the roadway has been paved over for pedestrian access only.

THE RAILWAY MUSEUM, FARINGDON ROAD
c1965 S254090

This building was originally built by the Great Western Railway as a lodging house for single men in 1846, and was called the Barracks. It was converted to a chapel for the Wesleyan Methodists by T S Lansdown of Swindon in 1869 - it could accommodate a congregation of 1,000. Closed in c1959, it became Swindon's Railway Museum in 1962 and remained as such until 1999. The new Steam Museum was opened in 2000. The building is now planned to be used by the New Mechanics' Institution Preservation Trust in their quest to restore this area of Swindon's railway heritage.

▶ FARINGDON ROAD PARK
c1965 S254104

The land for this park, west of the GWR Village, was donated in 1844 by Colonel T Vilett, one of the major landowners in the area, for the use of the railway community as a cricket ground and amenity area. Many famous cricketers played here in Victorian days, including Dr W G Grace. From 1868 it was the site for the famous annual children's fete, which continued until the outbreak of World War II. This social occasion, held on the second Saturday in August, attracted large crowds and required a large group of helpers to organize the catering, dances, tickets and admissions. In the foreground of this photograph are the remains of the formal Victorian gardens.

OUT OF TOWN

CRICKLADE ROAD *c1965* S254071
Looking South

This photograph shows the wide carriageway of Cricklade Road leading to Stratton Crossroads, with the junction of Beechcroft Road to the left and Whitworth Road to the right. The large shopping precinct to the right on the corner of Whitworth Road, Clive Parade, had been built circa 1960. Today, the crossroads is the site of one of Swindon's busiest mini-roundabout systems.

HEADLANDS GRAMMAR SCHOOL
c1965 S254082

This view, looking north over the playing fields, shows Headlands Grammar School, which had opened on this site in 1952 in Headlands Grove. Headlands School was originally formed in 1943 by the amalgamation of two secondary schools in the centre of the town, the College Secondary School and Euclid Street Secondary School, which continued to use both buildings until the new school was opened. In 1965, like many other grammar schools, Headlands was reorganized as a senior high school on the comprehensive basis, but it later lost its sixth form.

PENHILL DRIVE *c1960* S254078

In 1951 the Borough of Swindon purchased Penhill Farm, which lay in the parish of Stratton St Margaret, just outside the borough boundary north of the town, for housing. The following year the boundary was extended to bring all the land acquired into the borough. This photograph looks north, and shows what became the focal point for the estate, with the branch library to the right on the corner of Corsham Road, and the parade of shops, including Bollom, dry cleaners. To the left we can just glimpse the Deers Leap, a public house which was opened here in 1958 by Mitchells & Butler of Birmingham.

THE WHITE HART, OXFORD ROAD
c1950 S254003

This public house at Stratton St Margaret owes its existence to the Wilts and Berks Canal which ran nearby. The original inn stood on the opposite side of the road, on the south-western corner of what is now the busy Oxford road into Swindon. The original building was demolished, and a new one built in 1937-38 on its present site. One of its most famous landlords since then has been Johnnie Stiles, whose band had brought prestige to the town when winning the All British Dance Band Championships in both 1948 and 1949. Standing on the A419 Swindon by-pass and A420 Oxford Road interchange, the pub was subsequently extended and modernized in 1982.

TOWNS AND VILLAGES AROUND SWINDON

BROAD HINTON, SWINDON ROAD
c1955 B377005

An autumnal scene on the road to Broad Hinton, a pretty downland village which is situated six miles south of Swindon just off the A4361 road to Avebury.

▼ **BROAD HINTON,** *The Post Office c1945* B377008

This is Post Office Lane, and the village post office was located in the cottage on the left for many years up until 1966. The public telephone inside was one of the earliest in the village – the number was Broad Hinton 2. These cottages are now called Marloes and Gable House.

▼ **BROAD HINTON,** *The School and Thatched Corner c1955* B377001

The Church of England Primary School, founded by Thomas Benet of Salthrop in 1743, has been part of village life for over 250 years. We can see the sign 'Church of England Controlled School' attached to the school gate. Note the cobbled Pitchens path to the right.

▲ **BROAD HINTON,** *The White Horse c1955* B377003

This hill figure cut in the chalk lies on the face of Hackpen Hill, to the right of
the road from Wootton Bassett to Marlborough, where it zigzags to climb the
hill. It was said to have been cut in 1838 to commemorate the coronation of
Queen Victoria by Henry Eatwell, parish clerk of Broad Hinton, assisted,
according to some accounts, by the local publican. It is approximately 90ft
square in size.

67

▼ **CHISELDON**

The Old Pike House c1960 C220010

The brick-built extension on the corner to the row of 18th-century cottages was added as a toll house when the road from Burderop was turnpiked in 1814. When the toll house was renovated, the base of a privy to seat two adults and a child was found! The enamel road sign is still in situ.

▶ **CHISELDON**

The Canney c1960 C220004

This short length of road off New Road has several reputedly Tudor cottages. It is all that remains of a lost road from Aldbourne, which used to cross this area before the vast changes that occurred in the village during the building of the Swindon, Marlborough & Andover Railway (later Midland & South Western Junction Railway). A path still follows the route of the old road between the groups of cottages to link these to the rest of the community of Chiseldon.

◀ CHISELDON
High Street c1960 C220009

In the foreground is the railway bridge, with the High Street to the rear stretching up to the junction of Church Street and Butts Road. Beyond the bridge to the left stood the railway station, which closed in 1961. Beyond the station stands the Elm Tree public house, which was thatched until it was rebuilt around 1909. During World War I, when the railway line was in constant use by the military, thousands of men with their horses and equipment passed through the station, and the landlord of the Elm Tree would take trays full of mugs of beer down to the platform when the trains stopped here. The stump of the old elm tree, after which the public house was named, still existed when this photograph was taken, but it has, of course, now long disappeared.

▶ CHISELDON
Holy Cross Church c1960
C220001

The church dates back to c1200, although traces of an earlier Saxon building which was granted to Hyde Abbey, Winchester, in 903 may still be traced. The north aisle is said to have been constructed from stones taken from the old church at Draycot, which was demolished in 1572. The interior contains many tablets to Georgian members of the Calley family of Burderop Park. The author and poet Richard Jefferies was married to Jessie Baden in this church in 1874.

▶ **OGBOURNE ST GEORGE**
High Street c1955
O57007

This village is near one of the highest points of the Marlborough downs, and has changed little over the years. Like its near neighbour Chiseldon, it had a station on the Midland & South Western Junction Railway, reputed to be one of the coldest places on the line in winter, until it closed in 1961.

◀ **OGBOURNE ST GEORGE**
The Church and the Manor House c1955 O57001

St George's church to the right has a 13th-century doorway and a chancel arch with no piers; much else is of the 15th century. The brass portraits of a lord and lady of the manor in the 16th century - Thomas Goddard in a long furred gown with his wife - may be seen on the floor of the church. At one time the building was ringed by great elm trees, now gone, sad to say. The Jacobean manor house to the left stands on the site of a Benedictine priory founded in c1149 by Maud of Wallingford. The date 1619 is on the east chimney stack.

▲ **WANBOROUGH,** *The Cottage Shop c1965* W260021

These cottages stand at the top of Pack Hill, near its junction with Church Road and Mayfield, in Upper Wanborough. The Cottage Shop was once a shoemaker's premises. It closed in the 1970s and is now a private house.

◀**WANBOROUGH**
The Harrow Inn, High Street c1965 W260018

The Harrow is the oldest public house in Wanborough, dating back to at least the 18th century. It was situated next to the former Wanborough Brewery, now demolished - a close of new houses has been erected on the site. A new sign has now replaced the harrow on the end wall of the pub.

▼ **WANBOROUGH, HIGH STREET** *c1965* W260016
Looking North-West

This part of the village is known as Lower Wanborough, and lies 3 miles east of Swindon. In the foreground is Shear's Farm, once the Axe & Compass public house which closed in 1907. The building is now two private cottages. The road to the right leads to Callas Hill and Foxhill.

► **CRICKLADE, HIGH STREET**
c1955 C300006
Looking South-West

On the left stands the Red Lion public house. On the right we can see the roof of the chancel of St Mary's church. Although the church was declared redundant in the 1970s, since 1984 it has been leased back to the local Roman Catholic congregation. The High Street was the site of the local cattle and corn market for many years; market day was the third Tuesday of each month. Markets were held here until 1944, when they were moved to the railway station yard, but they were finally abandoned in 1953.

◀ **CRICKLADE** *c1955*
C300007
Looking from Cirencester Road into High Street

This photograph, taken from near the High Bridge over the River Thames, shows the entrance to Cricklade from the north. Immediately on the left is the unmistakable Victorian frontage of John Pater's School, known to generations of Cricklade people as 'the bottom school'. Ahead, in the High Street, stands the Red Lion inn.

▶ **HIGHWORTH,** *Swindon Street c1950* H157012
Looking South

The Co-op store on the left was previously a double-fronted residential property (today the windows are gone, and the shop has been taken into a new Co-op store which replaced the other adjacent buildings to its left). The outside gate to the shop is leaning against the wall to the left ready to be locked in place when the shop closes. The bus queue to Swindon is forming by the two lime trees outside Ashman's butchers shop, today a private house. Further down the street we can just see the sign for the Fishes public house.

HIGHWORTH, *High Street c1955* H157021 *Looking West*

This photograph was taken from near the King and Queen public house, possibly Highworth's oldest pub - it dates back to the 1600s. The gable-fronted building on the centre right was formerly another inn, the Cross Keys (now a fish and chip shop). Fred Croome's shop (right) is now a unisex hair salon. Facing us up the road in Swindon Street stands the early 18th-century Jesmond House Hotel.

HIGHWORTH, *High Street c1955*
H157002
Looking North-East

The grocer's shop (today a travel agents), on the left, carries the usual local notices in the window. On this quiet summer's day in the 1950s there was little traffic, allowing the young lady to take her ease sitting on the back of the horse-drawn delivery cart by the pavement! Behind the building we can see the tower of St Michael's church. This was held for King Charles I during the English Civil War, but it was stormed by the parliamentary commander Fairfax and his troops. The fallen soldiers were buried in a field near by, and the tower of the church was hit by a cannon ball.

HIGHWORTH, SHEEP STREET *c1955* H157011
Looking West

On the left the former Rifleman's Arms, then a private house, occupies the corner in the Market Square. This was later demolished, and today is a raised area with seats. Nearly opposite to this inn stands the Globe, another public house, which dates back to at least 1674, and the Red Lion, then an Ushers house, which closed in 1970. It is now offices. The building immediately to the right was then the offices of Percy Chick (Builders) Ltd. It was originally the Swan Inn, but it had closed by 1871.

HIGHWORTH,
The Market Square c1955
H157013
Looking East

This was the site for the town's livestock market for nearly seven hundred years and the centre for civic celebrations. Some years ago, however, the market committee sold the square to the local council for a nominal fee. The shop behind the parked Kemps van is now the Highworth Emporium, gifts and toys. To the right is the High Street, with the Saracen's Head Hotel, still with its illuminated sign, which had been introduced by Arkell's Brewery in the late 1930s. The hotel was renovated in 1966.

WOOTTON BASSETT, *High Street c1965* W171036

The wide High Street extends for about half a mile. On the left stands the Angel Hotel of chequered brick, which dates from the 18th century. The hotel was later completely modernized in 1989. As in Cricklade, the main street was the scene for the monthly livestock market, which was held on Wednesdays for many years. This continued until c1938, when the market was closed.

WOOTTON BASSETT
High Street c1950
W171010
Looking North-East

This view was taken slightly further from the south-west than photograph W171036 (previous page). The frontage of the Angel Hotel is hidden by a tree at the centre of the photograph. To the far left is Strange's Central Garage with a petrol pump outside. Its workshops were reached through the side entrance. Next to the garage stands the building contractors, decorators, ironmongers and funeral directors, Trow & Sons. Parking problems did not exist here in these days in the High Street.

WOOTTON BASSETT
The Town Hall c1950 W171012

The Town Hall, standing in the middle of the High Street, was given by Lawrence Hyde, first Earl of Rochester, in 1700. Restored in 1889, it was presented to the town by Lady Meux in 1906. Until the restoration in 1889, under the open staircase there was a lock-up or blind house. At one time the building was used as a court house; it has subsequently been used as a branch of the County Library and as a museum. In recent years it was restored with the help of English Heritage, initially in an overall grey finish, but it has since been restored to its traditional timber-framed look.

WOOTTON BASSETT
High Street and the Town Hall c1950 W171003

Looking north-east, this photograph shows a strangely deserted High Street. On the right is the junction with Station Road. Under the Town Hall once stood an old 18th-century fire engine with wooden wheels, and also the old stocks. The fire engine is now restored and in private hands, but the stocks are in the Town Hall Museum.

WOOTTON BASSETT
The Church and the Town Hall c1955 W171024

This photograph shows the junction of the High Street with Wood Street to the right. We can see the squat tower of St Bartholomew and All Saints' church rising over the roofs. Note the railings underneath the Town Hall, which have now been removed. The corner house on the end of Wood Street was restored to match the Town Hall in the restoration of 1889.

▼ **WOOTTON BASSETT,** *Station Road c1955* W171023

To the left stands the National School, built in 1860 by a local builder, Isaac Lansdown, on land given by Lord Clarendon; it was opened by the Bishop of Salisbury in August 1861. It was closed as a school in the 1970s, and is now the Wootton Bassett Civic Centre.

▼ **WOOTTON BASSETT,** *The Parish Church of St. Bartholomew and All Saints c1955* W171018

This 13th-century church was much restored and remodelled in 1869-71. It has a squat tower, about 40ft high, which was rebuilt at a cost of about £7,000. The ceiling of the nave was painted with a thousand stars. A new clock was installed in the tower in 1884, paid for by public subscription.

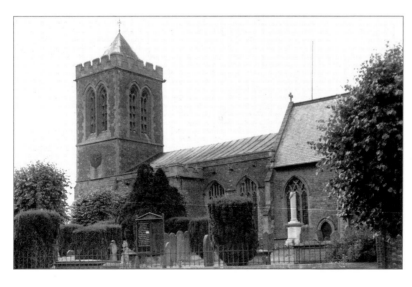

▲**WOOTTON BASSETT,** *High Street c1955* W171016

We are looking south west. This portion of the High Street sloping down to
Bath Road is known as Mount Pleasant.

WOOTTON BASSETT, *Bath Road c1950* W171009
Looking South-West

Here we see the cross roads, with New Road to Marlborough
on the left, and Whitehill Lane to Brinkworth on the right. On
the corner stands Herring's general store. The shop is now a
private house.

Acknowledgements

The author would like to thank David Bedford for his invaluable help in
compiling this book. Thanks also to Roy Burbidge, Dennis Harber,
Walter Ineson, Beryl Macdonald and the staff of Swindon Reference Library.

INDEX

Frith Book Co Titles

www.francisfrith.co.uk

The Frith Book Company publishes over 100 new titles each year. A selection of those currently available are listed below. For latest catalogue please contact Frith Book Co.
Town Books 96 pages, approximately 100 photos. **County and Themed Books** 128 pages, approximately 150 photos (unless specified). All titles hardback with laminated case and jacket, except those indicated pb (paperback)

Amersham, Chesham & Rickmansworth (pb)	1-85937-340-2	£9.99	Devon (pb)	1-85937-297-x	£9.99
Andover (pb)	1-85937-292-9	£9.99	Devon Churches (pb)	1-85937-250-3	£9.99
Aylesbury (pb)	1-85937-227-9	£9.99	Dorchester (pb)	1-85937-307-0	£9.99
Barnstaple (pb)	1-85937-300-3	£9.99	Dorset (pb)	1-85937-269-4	£9.99
Basildon Living Memories (pb)	1-85937-515-4	£9.99	Dorset Coast (pb)	1-85937-299-6	£9.99
Bath (pb)	1-85937-419-0	£9.99	Dorset Living Memories (pb)	1-85937-584-7	£9.99
Bedford (pb)	1-85937-205-8	£9.99	Down the Severn (pb)	1-85937-560-x	£9.99
Bedfordshire Living Memories	1-85937-513-8	£14.99	Down The Thames (pb)	1-85937-278-3	£9.99
Belfast (pb)	1-85937-303-8	£9.99	Down the Trent	1-85937-311-9	£14.99
Berkshire (pb)	1-85937-191-4	£9.99	East Anglia (pb)	1-85937-265-1	£9.99
Berkshire Churches	1-85937-170-1	£17.99	East Grinstead (pb)	1-85937-138-8	£9.99
Berkshire Living Memories	1-85937-332-1	£14.99	East London	1-85937-080-2	£14.99
Black Country	1-85937-497-2	£12.99	East Sussex (pb)	1-85937-606-1	£9.99
Blackpool (pb)	1-85937-393-3	£9.99	Eastbourne (pb)	1-85937-399-2	£9.99
Bognor Regis (pb)	1-85937-431-x	£9.99	Edinburgh (pb)	1-85937-193-0	£8.99
Bournemouth (pb)	1-85937-545-6	£9.99	England In The 1880s	1-85937-331-3	£17.99
Bradford (pb)	1-85937-204-x	£9.99	Essex - Second Selection	1-85937-456-5	£14.99
Bridgend (pb)	1-85937-386-0	£7.99	Essex (pb)	1-85937-270-8	£9.99
Bridgwater (pb)	1-85937-305-4	£9.99	Essex Coast	1-85937-342-9	£14.99
Bridport (pb)	1-85937-327-5	£9.99	Essex Living Memories	1-85937-490-5	£14.99
Brighton (pb)	1-85937-192-2	£8.99	Exeter	1-85937-539-1	£9.99
Bristol (pb)	1-85937-264-3	£9.99	Exmoor (pb)	1-85937-608-8	£9.99
British Life A Century Ago (pb)	1-85937-213-9	£9.99	Falmouth (pb)	1-85937-594-4	£9.99
Buckinghamshire (pb)	1-85937-200-7	£9.99	Folkestone (pb)	1-85937-124-8	£9.99
Camberley (pb)	1-85937-222-8	£9.99	Frome (pb)	1-85937-317-8	£9.99
Cambridge (pb)	1-85937-422-0	£9.99	Glamorgan	1-85937-488-3	£14.99
Cambridgeshire (pb)	1-85937-420-4	£9.99	Glasgow (pb)	1-85937-190-6	£9.99
Cambridgeshire Villages	1-85937-523-5	£14.99	Glastonbury (pb)	1-85937-338-0	£7.99
Canals And Waterways (pb)	1-85937-291-0	£9.99	Gloucester (pb)	1-85937-232-5	£9.99
Canterbury Cathedral (pb)	1-85937-179-5	£9.99	Gloucestershire (pb)	1-85937-561-8	£9.99
Cardiff (pb)	1-85937-093-4	£9.99	Great Yarmouth (pb)	1-85937-426-3	£9.99
Carmarthenshire (pb)	1-85937-604-5	£9.99	Greater Manchester (pb)	1-85937-266-x	£9.99
Chelmsford (pb)	1-85937-310-0	£9.99	Guildford (pb)	1-85937-410-7	£9.99
Cheltenham (pb)	1-85937-095-0	£9.99	Hampshire (pb)	1-85937-279-1	£9.99
Cheshire (pb)	1-85937-271-6	£9.99	Harrogate (pb)	1-85937-423-9	£9.99
Chester (pb)	1-85937-382 8	£9.99	Hastings and Bexhill (pb)	1-85937-131-0	£9.99
Chesterfield (pb)	1-85937-378-x	£9.99	Heart of Lancashire (pb)	1-85937-197-3	£9.99
Chichester (pb)	1-85937-228-7	£9.99	Helston (pb)	1-85937-214-7	£9.99
Churches of East Cornwall (pb)	1-85937-249-x	£9.99	Hereford (pb)	1-85937-175-2	£9.99
Churches of Hampshire (pb)	1-85937-207-4	£9.99	Herefordshire (pb)	1-85937-567-7	£9.99
Cinque Ports & Two Ancient Towns	1-85937-492-1	£14.99	Herefordshire Living Memories	1-85937-514-6	£14.99
Colchester (pb)	1-85937-188-4	£8.99	Hertfordshire (pb)	1-85937-247-3	£9.99
Cornwall (pb)	1-85937-229-5	£9.99	Horsham (pb)	1-85937-432-8	£9.99
Cornwall Living Memories	1-85937-248-1	£14.99	Humberside (pb)	1-85937-605-3	£9.99
Cotswolds (pb)	1-85937-230-9	£9.99	Hythe, Romney Marsh, Ashford (pb)	1-85937-256-2	£9.99
Cotswolds Living Memories	1-85937-255-4	£14.99	Ipswich (pb)	1-85937-424-7	£9.99
County Durham (pb)	1-85937-398-4	£9.99	Isle of Man (pb)	1-85937-268-6	£9.99
Croydon Living Memories (pb)	1-85937-162-0	£9.99	Isle of Wight (pb)	1-85937-429-8	£9.99
Cumbria (pb)	1-85937-621-5	£9.99	Isle of Wight Living Memories	1-85937-304-6	£14.99
Derby (pb)	1-85937-367-4	£9.99	Kent (pb)	1-85937-189-2	£9.99
Derbyshire (pb)	1-85937-196-5	£9.99	Kent Living Memories(pb)	1-85937-401-8	£9.99
Derbyshire Living Memories	1-85937-330-5	£14.99	Kings Lynn (pb)	1-85937-334-8	£9.99

Available from your local bookshop or from the publisher

Frith Book Co Titles (continued)

Title	ISBN	Price		Title	ISBN	Price
Lake District (pb)	1-85937-275-9	£9.99		Sherborne (pb)	1-85937-301-1	£9.99
Lancashire Living Memories	1-85937-335-6	£14.99		Shrewsbury (pb)	1-85937-325-9	£9.99
Lancaster, Morecambe, Heysham (pb)	1-85937-233-3	£9.99		Shropshire (pb)	1-85937-326-7	£9.99
Leeds (pb)	1-85937-202-3	£9.99		Shropshire Living Memories	1-85937-643-6	£14.99
Leicester (pb)	1-85937-381-x	£9.99		Somerset	1-85937-153-1	£14.99
Leicestershire & Rutland Living Memories	1-85937-500-6	£12.99		South Devon Coast	1-85937-107-8	£14.99
Leicestershire (pb)	1-85937-185-x	£9.99		South Devon Living Memories (pb)	1-85937-609-6	£9.99
Lighthouses	1-85937-257-0	£9.99		South East London (pb)	1-85937-263-5	£9.99
Lincoln (pb)	1-85937-380-1	£9.99		South Somerset	1-85937-318-6	£14.99
Lincolnshire (pb)	1-85937-433-6	£9.99		South Wales	1-85937-519-7	£14.99
Liverpool and Merseyside (pb)	1-85937-234-1	£9.99		Southampton (pb)	1-85937-427-1	£9.99
London (pb)	1-85937-183-3	£9.99		Southend (pb)	1-85937-313-5	£9.99
London Living Memories	1-85937-454-9	£14.99		Southport (pb)	1-85937-425-5	£9.99
Ludlow (pb)	1-85937-176-0	£9.99		St Albans (pb)	1-85937-341-0	£9.99
Luton (pb)	1-85937-235-x	£9.99		St Ives (pb)	1-85937-415-8	£9.99
Maidenhead (pb)	1-85937-339-9	£9.99		Stafford Living Memories (pb)	1-85937-503-0	£9.99
Maidstone (pb)	1-85937-391-7	£9.99		Staffordshire (pb)	1-85937-308-9	£9.99
Manchester (pb)	1-85937-198-1	£9.99		Stourbridge (pb)	1-85937-530-8	£9.99
Marlborough (pb)	1-85937-336-4	£9.99		Stratford upon Avon (pb)	1-85937-388-7	£9.99
Middlesex	1-85937-158-2	£14.99		Suffolk (pb)	1-85937-221-x	£9.99
Monmouthshire	1-85937-532-4	£14.99		Suffolk Coast (pb)	1-85937-610-x	£9.99
New Forest (pb)	1-85937-390-9	£9.99		Surrey (pb)	1-85937-240-6	£9.99
Newark (pb)	1-85937-366-6	£9.99		Surrey Living Memories	1-85937-328-3	£14.99
Newport, Wales (pb)	1-85937-258-9	£9.99		Sussex (pb)	1-85937-184-1	£9.99
Newquay (pb)	1-85937-421-2	£9.99		Sutton (pb)	1-85937-337-2	£9.99
Norfolk (pb)	1-85937-195-7	£9.99		Swansea (pb)	1-85937-167-1	£9.99
Norfolk Broads	1-85937-486-7	£14.99		Taunton (pb)	1-85937-314-3	£9.99
Norfolk Living Memories (pb)	1-85937-402-6	£9.99		Tees Valley & Cleveland (pb)	1-85937-623-1	£9.99
North Buckinghamshire	1-85937-626-6	£14.99		Teignmouth (pb)	1-85937-370-4	£7.99
North Devon Living Memories	1-85937-261-9	£14.99		Thanet (pb)	1-85937-116-7	£9.99
North Hertfordshire	1-85937-547-2	£14.99		Tiverton (pb)	1-85937-178-7	£9.99
North London (pb)	1-85937-403-4	£9.99		Torbay (pb)	1-85937-597-9	£9.99
North Somerset	1-85937-302-x	£14.99		Truro (pb)	1-85937-598-7	£9.99
North Wales (pb)	1-85937-298-8	£9.99		Victorian & Edwardian Dorset	1-85937-254-6	£14.99
North Yorkshire (pb)	1-85937-236-8	£9.99		Victorian & Edwardian Kent (pb)	1-85937-624-X	£9.99
Northamptonshire Living Memories	1-85937-529-4	£14.99		Victorian & Edwardian Maritime Album (pb)	1-85937-622-3	£9.99
Northamptonshire	1-85937-150-7	£14.99		Victorian and Edwardian Sussex (pb)	1-85937-625-8	£9.99
Northumberland Tyne & Wear (pb)	1-85937-281-3	£9.99		Villages of Devon (pb)	1-85937-293-7	£9.99
Northumberland	1-85937-522-7	£14.99		Villages of Kent (pb)	1-85937-294-5	£9.99
Norwich (pb)	1-85937-194-9	£8.99		Villages of Sussex (pb)	1-85937-295-3	£9.99
Nottingham (pb)	1-85937-324-0	£9.99		Warrington (pb)	1-85937-507-3	£9.99
Nottinghamshire (pb)	1-85937-187-6	£9.99		Warwick (pb)	1-85937-518-9	£9.99
Oxford (pb)	1-85937-411-5	£9.99		Warwickshire (pb)	1-85937-203-1	£9.99
Oxfordshire (pb)	1-85937-430-1	£9.99		Welsh Castles (pb)	1-85937-322-4	£9.99
Oxfordshire Living Memories	1-85937-525-1	£14.99		West Midlands (pb)	1-85937-289-9	£9.99
Paignton (pb)	1-85937-374-7	£7.99		West Sussex (pb)	1-85937-607-x	£9.99
Peak District (pb)	1-85937-280-5	£9.99		West Yorkshire (pb)	1-85937-201-5	£9.99
Pembrokeshire	1-85937-262-7	£14.99		Weston Super Mare (pb)	1-85937-306-2	£9.99
Penzance (pb)	1-85937-595-2	£9.99		Weymouth (pb)	1-85937-209-0	£9.99
Peterborough (pb)	1-85937-219-8	£9.99		Wiltshire (pb)	1-85937-277-5	£9.99
Picturesque Harbours	1-85937-208-2	£14.99		Wiltshire Churches (pb)	1-85937-171-x	£9.99
Piers	1-85937-237-6	£17.99		Wiltshire Living Memories (pb)	1-85937-396-8	£9.99
Plymouth (pb)	1-85937-389-5	£9.99		Winchester (pb)	1-85937-428-x	£9.99
Poole & Sandbanks (pb)	1-85937-251-1	£9.99		Windsor (pb)	1-85937-333-x	£9.99
Preston (pb)	1-85937-212-0	£9.99		Wokingham & Bracknell (pb)	1-85937-329-1	£9.99
Reading (pb)	1-85937-238-4	£9.99		Woodbridge (pb)	1-85937-498-0	£9.99
Redhill to Reigate (pb)	1-85937-596-0	£9.99		Worcester (pb)	1-85937-165-5	£9.99
Ringwood (pb)	1-85937-384-4	£7.99		Worcestershire Living Memories	1-85937-489-1	£14.99
Romford (pb)	1-85937-319-4	£9.99		Worcestershire	1-85937-152-3	£14.99
Royal Tunbridge Wells (pb)	1-85937-504-9	£9.99		York (pb)	1-85937-199-x	£9.99
Salisbury (pb)	1-85937-239-2	£9.99		Yorkshire (pb)	1-85937-186-8	£9.99
Scarborough (pb)	1-85937-379-8	£9.99		Yorkshire Coastal Memories	1-85937-506-5	£14.99
Sevenoaks and Tonbridge (pb)	1-85937-392-5	£9.99		Yorkshire Dales	1-85937-502-2	£14.99
Sheffield & South Yorks (pb)	1-85937-267-8	£9.99		Yorkshire Living Memories (pb)	1-85937-397-6	£9.99

See Frith books on the internet at www.francisfrith.co.uk

FRITH PRODUCTS & SERVICES

Francis Frith would doubtless be pleased to know that the pioneering publishing venture he started in 1860 still continues today. Over a hundred and forty years later, The Francis Frith Collection continues in the same innovative tradition and is now one of the foremost publishers of vintage photographs in the world. Some of the current activities include:

Interior Decoration

Today Frith's photographs can be seen framed and as giant wall murals in thousands of pubs, restaurants, hotels, banks, retail stores and other public buildings throughout the country. In every case they enhance the unique local atmosphere of the places they depict and provide reminders of gentler days in an increasingly busy and frenetic world.

Product Promotions

Frith products are used by many major companies to promote the sales of their own products or to reinforce their own history and heritage. Frith promotions have been used by Hovis bread, Courage beers, Scots Porage Oats, Colman's mustard, Cadbury's foods, Mellow Birds coffee, Dunhill pipe tobacco, Guinness, and Bulmer's Cider.

Genealogy and Family History

As the interest in family history and roots grows world-wide, more and more people are turning to Frith's photographs of Great Britain for images of the towns, villages and streets where their ancestors lived; and, of course, photographs of the churches and chapels where their ancestors were christened, married and buried are an essential part of every genealogy tree and family album.

Frith Products

All Frith photographs are available Framed or just as Mounted Prints and Posters (size 23 x 16 inches). These may be ordered from the address below. From time to time other products - Address Books, Calendars, Table Mats, etc - are available.

The Internet

Already fifty thousand Frith photographs can be viewed and purchased on the internet through the Frith websites and a myriad of partner sites.

For more detailed information on Frith companies and products, look at these sites:

www.francisfrith.co.uk
www.francisfrith.com
(for North American visitors)

See the complete list of Frith Books at:

www.francisfrith.co.uk

This web site is regularly updated with the latest list of publications from the Frith Book Company. If you wish to buy books relating to another part of the country that your local bookshop does not stock, you may purchase on-line.

For further information, trade, or author enquiries please contact us at the address below:
The Francis Frith Collection, Frith's Barn, Teffont, Salisbury, Wiltshire, England SP3 5QP.
Tel: +44 (0)1722 716 376 Fax: +44 (0)1722 716 881 Email: sales@francisfrith.co.uk

See Frith books on the internet at www.francisfrith.co.uk